CONTENTS

NOTE TO THE THIRD EDITION

This new edition has been revised here and there in the light of earlier readers' comments. I'm grateful to all these readers, and to the publishers for their generous patience while I worked.

The content and argument are unchanged.

I've recast the preface, and condensed my treatment of Leviticus. Some readers have told me that I assumed too much basic knowledge of Christianity: in response to these I've recast the sections that cover the Genesis creation-myths and the first chapter of Romans, and added a couple of explanatory Notes, one on the terminology and structure of the Christian churches and one on the layout of the Bible. But this self-defence manual is still intended to be read side-by-side with a copy of the Bible, in one or more of its many versions.

Homophobia and the Bible

A Self-Defence Manual

Michael Halls

ISBN 1 902706 00 5

Published by

IN OTHER WORDS
PUBLISHING

In Other Words Ltd
64 Mutley Plain Plymouth PL4 6LF
Tel: +44 (0) 1 752 663889 Fax: +44 (0) 1 752 252 232
email: info@ inotherwordspublishing.co.uk
www.inotherwordspublishing.co.uk

PREFACE

I have written this booklet for gay people who are not Christians. I have also done all I could to make it accessible to any other readers who may be interested. Its contents are not in any sense new. I have summed up basic knowledge available to anyone who can make time to do some reading. But the facts are accurate and reliable: though this is hardly a wild boast when one's opponents are people capable of confusing תֶּבֶל with תּוֹעֵבָה , and πόρνοι with κύνες .[1]

There is a certain kind of homophobic aggression that is specially difficult for its victims to confront: I mean the bigotry that exploits the language of revealed religion. This language is both emotive and very technical, and it has an automatic authority for certain tabloid audiences. People who would never dream of studying the Bible for themselves, and who go to Church only to be hatched, matched and dispatched, still listen when they hear the words "the Bible says"—especially when what follows is something they're glad to hear. And the language of biblical exegesis and moral theology sounds so impressively technical that few interviewers have the confidence or the expertise to challenge the speakers, though a good deal of what they say about doctrine and about the Bible is in fact quite untrue.

Readers who have encountered these people in the pub, or on television, or on radio phone-ins, will understand why we need to have defences against them. Populist aggression, deep-rooted factual error, an open sectarian hatred, a dogmatic implacability, and a pseudo-pastoral manipulativeness... this is a combination which arouses in genuine Christians, as it should in all of us, a sense of deep dismay. I hope that something here might help to redress the balance of power by providing the ordinary gay man and woman in the pub with material which could make discussions less unequal.

I also hope that this booklet might offer useful support to those gay people within the Church who are vulnerable to the sly insinuation that their sexuality might be a kind of hurdle which some strange, morally alien deity is watching them trying to leap.This doctrine of "renunciatory celibacy" is not only false doctrine, but also psychological abuse. It can do—has done—great harm. Whatever our orientation, we know that our sexuality is the deepest wellspring. of our selfhood, of our sense of our own being. It is not only morally wrong, it is psychologically and spiritually dangerous to poison this wellspring.[2]

There is another strand to modern bigotry, the idea that homosexuality is in some way biologically 'unnatural' or 'not normal', and that social disapproval, combined with legislation, can somehow discourage it. I have largely ignored this. It is evident nonsense, as history vividly shows: all that bigotry, prejudice and discrimination do is spread misery and encourage genuine and shameful social evils such as self-harm, substance-abuse, and suicide. It is also irrelevant to this booklet, since the principal churches now agree that same-gender love

I

and sex are natural to the human species. The issue, as they describe it nowadays, is not the biological, but the doctrinal status of homosexuality.

Nevertheless, there are still a few who wish to persuade us that homosexuality is 'unnatural'. They talk as if it is *only* the result of environmental influences, influences which can *always* be reversed. These are the sad aggressive people who use the word 'cure'. In this context, the word 'cure' is both meaningless and unwholesome: you cannot 'cure' someone of being in good health. The existence of gay people is a clear and wonderful demonstration of the valuable and positive diversity of human nature, and those people who, out of their own private needs, want to persuade us it is some kind of environmentally-imposed dysfunction have all history and all experience against them. They have not yet even shown that they know how any such case might be presented.[3]

Some non-Christian readers will wish I hadn't gone into so much arcane detail; some Christians will feel I have included too much that is elementary. I apologise in all directions: it's difficult to address two audiences simultaneously. Having left the Church myself long ago, after many years of strongly committed devotion, I can still remember how all-encompassing one's fulfilment can be when one is inside. I can also remember my new sense of fulfilment and relief when I—as I perceived it—escaped. I don't undervalue either of these, and this booklet does not take sides. If I have failed to avoid giving offence to any Christians whose doubts about homosexuality are purely doctrinal, and have no element of personal homophobia, I am deeply sorry: that would be a failure of my dialectical resources, not of my will.

This booklet isn't merely a matter of self-defence, and its contents are of living importance to all of us, whatever our orientation. Bigotry and sectarian abuse are absolute evils, and damage the whole of society. And we need to be able to offer practical support to those around us: our own children, perhaps; our brothers and sisters, parents, our partner, neighbours, pupils, co-workers, friends or fellow-students. We all know how life can be darkened, and sometimes prematurely ended, by social prejudice; and like all forms of prejudice, this warped religious bigotry breeds discrimination, misery, violence, and self-harm.

Above all, too many have died. Too many families and friends have had to endure this senseless, almost unimaginable loss, and will never again be whole.

NOTES

1   For *tevel* and *to`evah* see **4.4.4** below. For *pornoi* and *kunes* see **5.4.3** and **5.8**.

2   "False doctrine", because this celibacy movement is not in fact rooted in orthodox Christianity. It is a new version of a peculiarly unpleasant mediæval heresy called Catharism. See **5.1.4** below.

3   A sad (or perhaps some would rather say, 'the only amusing') feature of the evangelical 'ex-gay' or 'cure' movement is to see people who call themselves

Bible Christians begging both bricks and straw from the very same manipulative behavioural psychologists whom they were denouncing, a mere thirty years ago, as godless perverters of the Christian doctrine of free will.

REFERENCES

Apart from the Preface, all the sections and paragraphs in this booklet are numbered. Internal cross-references to these section and paragraph numbers are printed in small bold letters, like this: **5.1.1.**

I have printed Bible references within square brackets *[Prov 8:7-8]*. For an explanation of how to look up Bible references, see the **Note on using the Bible** at the end.

BIBLE VERSIONS and ABBREVIATIONS

DR: the Douay-Rheims translation, 1582-1609 (Roman Catholic)
GNB: the Good News Bible,1966
JB: the Jerusalem Bible, 1968
  NJB: the New Jerusalem Bible, 1985 (the **JB** revised and partially corrected)
KJV: the King James or Authorised Version, 1611 (Church of England)
NEB: the New English Bible, 1961-70
  REB: the Revised English Bible, 1989 (the **NEB** revised and partially corrected) ·
NIV: the New International Version, 1988
RSV: the Revised Standard Version, 1952

There are many other populist modern English versions (e.g. the Living Bible and the Amplified Bible) but most of these have been so freely rewritten by their 'translators' that they hardly correspond to the original Bible at all. Pointing out their errors, let alone their bigotry, is as mechanical as shooting tin cans, but it takes an awful amount of space. I've ignored them. Readers who care to can look them up and assess them for themselves in the light of what they read in this booklet.

Basic resources for those who want to study the original Hebrew and Greek are:

R. Kittel, edd. K. Elliger & W. Rudolph, *Biblica Hebraica Stuttgartensia* (Stuttgart 1966-77)
G. Lisowsky & L. Rost, *Konkordanz zum Hebräischen Alten Testament* (2nd edition, 1966)
F. Brown, S.R. Driver & C.A. Briggs, *A Hebrew and English Lexicon of the Old Testament* (Oxford 1907; rev. edn 1966)
B. Einspahr, *Index to Brown, Driver & Briggs Hebrew Lexicon* (London 1976)
A. Rahlfs, *Septuaginta* (Stuttgart, 1935)
J. Ziegler, J.W. Wevers et al., *Septuaginta: Vetus Testamentum Graecum* (Göttingen, 1936-; continuing)
K. Aland, *The Greek New Testament*, United Bible Societies (3rd edition, Stuttgart 1983)
H.G. Liddell and R. Scott, *A Greek-English Lexicon* (1843; 9th edn with supplement, Oxford 1968)

W.F. Arndt & F.W. Gingrich, *A Greek-English Lexicon of the New Testament and Other Early Christian Literature* (Cambridge 1957)

R. Young, *Analytical Concordance to the Holy Bible* (1879; 8th edn, London 1939)

People who use Lexicons and Concordances and Bible Commentaries should be on their guard. All these books reflect the prejudices and preconceptions of their authors, and of their period in history. For instance, even Liddell & Scott's great Greek Lexicon is still largely based on old mediæval word-lists.

1   CHRISTIANITY IN THE 1990s: THE STATE OF PLAY

1.1   No Consensus

It's important to remember that the homophobes do not represent some kind of united consensus of the Church. There is no such consensus. There never was. Many Christians condemn not only the homophobes' general opinions, but specifically the way they use the Bible.

1.2   Not sticking to its traditions

An oppressive anxiety about sexuality is not a permanent condition of the Church. In its earliest years, nearest the time of Jesus, the Church appears not to have been institutionally homophobic at all (see section **6** below); and this current phase is hardly five years old. Many older gays and lesbians will remember that in the years 1950 to 1980, when British social homophobia reached its nastiest depths, there were both Protestant and Catholic congregations which offered them a kind of sanctuary. Even some widely-respected evangelicals believed that what their congregation got up to in the bedroom was a matter for private consciences, and no business of the Church, and said in private that in terms of moral theology the whole question had become a dead letter.

The complaint that there are now, in the 1990s, many gay clergy does not imply a recent loosening of moral standards in the Church. Rather, the complaint itself demonstrates a falling off from a period when the Church, true to its oldest traditions, quietly made Christian space for those whom a secular and bigoted society was persecuting.

Like all phases, this too will pass.

1.3   Not averse to sex

There's a long and honourable tradition of celebrating sexual joy in the Church, reaching back 2,500 years to the Old Testament book called the Song of Songs. This is unarguably a part of the Bible. It is also one of the most vivid, most ecstatically happy, and most sexually explicit erotic poems ever written.

> "—What spells lie in your love, my sister, my promised bride! ..The curve of your thighs is like the curve of a necklace.. Your breasts are two fawns.."

> "—Ah, why are you not my brother, nursed at my mother's breast! Then if I met you out of doors, I could kiss you without people thinking ill of me."

Song of Songs, 4:10, 7:1,3, 8:1. *JB*

People whose faith centres on a puritan dislike of sex in general are hardly in the main stream of Christianity.

1.4   The denial of love

Puritans tend to insist that discussions of sexuality must always begin from and circle round questions of physical sexual activity. Now whatever our orientation or beliefs may be, this attitude diminishes us all: it is a terrible denial of love. Some people in particular appear to be single-mindedly obsessed with anal sex. They seem to believe that all homosexual men express their love this way, and that no heterosexuals do. They are wrong, of course, on both counts, but they can become strangely disturbed when you point this out. Whatever they may say about the Bible, this particular strain of homophobia often seems to spring from some purely personal obsession or dysfunction.

1.5   Damaging inconsistency

However much the doctrines of the different Christian groups conflict with one another, all the groups claim that their doctrines are derived from the Bible, and differ only because they use different rules for interpreting what it contains. Interpretation, they agree, is essential. If we did not distinguish the living doctrine from the undergrowth of dead taboos, it would be, for example, for one whole year out of every seven years, a sin to weed the garden.[1] But when the homophobes are challenged about their homophobia, they suddenly reverse their position and insist that on this one subject the Bible is quite different—we must not interpret the surface text at all—we have to read it with a flat, unthinking literalness. Obviously this position is indefensible. But things get worse, for (as we shall see below) the surface text they point to is misleadingly translated, and leads them astray.

1.6   The basic challenge

There are many Christians who are not puritans, and some of these also believe that the Bible condemns homosexuality. It is right to ask them where, and also to remind them, first, that many other Christians, past and present, disagree with them; and second, that their personal beliefs have no authority over others.

1.7   No general moral authority

Whatever the Bible is, it is not a book of laws for non-Christians. Its spiritual authority—its claim to contain truths that we cannot know except by divine revelation—exists only for believers. Where the Bible seems to say things that non-Christians do not believe to be morally or socially good, or true, or even humane, we have every right to think these things over on their merits, or turn the page, or put the book aside. The apostle St Paul laid down rules by which Christians may judge each other's behaviour *[1 Cor 5:9-13]*, but they should *not*, he states, pass judgement on the behaviour of the people they live amongst.

The great moral theologian St Augustine took this distinction between people inside and outside the Church to an interesting extreme. In his book *About Married Bliss* he instructed Christian women whose husbands like to perform non-procreative sex (e.g. buggery) to send them off to relieve their needs with (pagan) prostitutes. [*De bono coniugali*, 11]

NOTES

1   Leviticus 25:1-7; see **3.1** below.

2 JESUS AND THE GOSPELS

2.1 The Silence of Jesus

Jesus himself, the founder of Christianity, made no criticism at all, at any time, of homosexuality or same-sex sexual behaviour.

For the followers of Jesus, this silence has weight. It was not due to ignorance. Same-sex sexual behaviour was familiar to the Jews (see below: **4.4** and **4.5**). Amongst the Romans, the rulers of Judæa at the time, it was regarded as a natural option within a normal sex-life, so long as it was consensual. (They gave same-sex marriages the same status as heterosexual marriages, but they had strict laws to punish rape and child-abuse.)

Jesus spoke freely about his contemporaries' moral and social behaviour, but never mentioned this. If he had wished to criticise any aspect of same-sex love or sexuality, let alone to forbid same-sex sex to his followers, three years of teaching gave him ample opportunity. **But he did not.**

2.2 "Family values"

Some homophobes argue that Jesus *implicitly* supported the political programme that they like to call 'traditional family values', and so he was therefore (also implicitly) hostile to homosexuality. But this repressive anti-gay 'family values' programme is modern, not traditional at all. It is therefore hardly surprising that the Bible contains no evidence that Jesus supported it. In fact, reading the Gospels, it is difficult not to notice that Jesus himself ran away from home *[Luke 2:41-52]* , never married, never worked for his living, publicly rejected his mother and his family's claims on him *[Mark 3:20-35]*, and vividly enjoined his disciples to be prepared to renounce their families too *[Matthew 10:35-37, Luke 14:26]*. And in general, Jesus was no advocate of social conformism or moral repressiveness.

2.3 "Christian marriage"

The 'traditional family values' people place immense emphasis on something they call 'Christian marriage', but what they are talking about is in fact a modern invention. It did not exist in the early Church, nor indeed for the first eleven hundred years of the Church's history. Marriage didn't even have the status of a sacrament till the Lateran Council of 1179. Before then, Christians got married in a secular legal ceremony, based on that used in pre-Christian days by the Romans, followed by a wedding-feast. To this could be added a simple religious blessing (either of the couple themselves or of the marriage-bed), which included prayers and an invocation of Christian patron saints. The ceremony did not have to take place in church.

The sacramental status of Protestant and Catholic marriage is odd. Some conservative theologians have called it anomalous. In important respects it does not even fit the canonical definition of a sacrament. Oddest of all, it is the only sacrament where the minister or priest has no power of performance. The couple being married are, technically, their own ministers or celebrants. The minister is there only to give the blessing *afterwards*, and to confirm publicly that a marriage *has been* performed. To see the minister's rôle in a marriage-service as equivalent to her/his rôle at Mass or Communion is to misunderstand the very nature of what is going on.

2.4   On behaving morally

Jesus's direct and positive teachings on behaviour have to do with love, personal integrity, the renunciation of physical and psychological violence, and our duty to honour and respect each other without prejudice. He left no comfort for those who would like Christianity to become a moralistic system of general social control.

2.5   On behaving moralistically

The best example that we can find in the Gospels of a pressure-group trying to impose their moralistic values on co-religionists who disagree with them seems to be that of Jesus's main enemies, the Pharisees.

3   THE BIBLE

So much for what Jesus didn't say. What is there in the Bible that the homophobes might point to?

3.1   What do we find in the Bible?

The Bible is not a simple unified list of clear transparent moral rules. Far from it. Its various books include a broad mixture of history, legislation, poetry, mythology, and much else. They were written and rewritten over a long period, at least nine hundred years, during which the society, lifestyle and languages of the Holy Land changed enormously. In some places we recognise principles that seem universal in human society, such as laws against murder, theft and fraud. We also find laws that only refer to a specific time, place, or nation, such as those that say that for one whole year out of every seven no-one may sow or harvest their fields, prune their vines, or pluck fruit *[Lev 25:1-7]*. Over the last two thousand years there has been a great deal of argument between different groups of Christians about exactly which of these rules are permanent and universal, and which have become obsolete. Different Christian Churches, and different groups within each Church, have arrived at massively different conclusions about how the Bible is to be interpreted and applied to modern life. There is no consensus. [1]

3.1.1   There have been many arguments over what is actually "in the Bible". The Protestant and Catholic churches still disagree over whether the Old Testament contains 46 books or only 39.

3.1.2   There is no single perfect and reliable copy of the Bible. For more than fifteen hundred years, before printing was invented, every new copy had to be written out by hand. Errors crept in at every stage. We know that sometimes, particularly in the New Testament, deliberate but unauthorised changes were made, so as to give support to a particular point of view. [2] New variations were inextricably mingled into subsequent copies. After all this, we cannot return to some kind of perfect 'original' text. The manuscripts that have survived differ too widely. (See, e.g. **5.4.4** below.) Behind the smooth authoritative surface of any translation lies a thicket of difficult alternatives.

3.1.3   Printing the Bible with numbered verses is a quite recent invention. It was not originally written that way. (The chapter-divisions are older, but are still not part of the writers' original text, and they can also be misleading.) People get magnetised by the contents of a single chapter, or single verse, without noticing that it is part of an argument. It is always important to evaluate the whole passage using a wide sample of different translations. At Romans 1, for instance, the homophobes seem to have absorbed little phrases here and there, but not the context—not what Paul is actually talking about. (See **5.1.2** below.)

3.1.4   In some versions the translators have portioned the text out into their own sections, each one headed with a kind of one-line summary of what the translators mean it to say. But there are no section-headings, and no marked section-breaks, in any version of the original text. Many of them are questionable. Some are misleading.

3.2 The languages of the Bible

Most of us cannot read the Bible itself: we have to rely on the work of translators. None of the Bible was written in English. The Old Testament has come down to us partly in Hebrew, partly in Greek. The New Testament survives only in Greek.

The vocabularies of ancient Greek and Hebrew reflect the differing societies of two distinct races that grew up eight hundred miles apart in a world which was almost unimaginably different from our own. Over the centuries much has been forgotten about these early civilisations and their languages. There are passages in the Bible that have been impenetrably obscure for centuries. Even the basic meaning of some words is now unknown and unretrievable. (For one important example see **5.3.2** below.)

3.2.1 Jesus himself used a language called Aramaic, but his original words have long been lost. Our only knowledge of what he said comes through the Greek translations of his words that we find in the Gospels. (Jesus himself never wrote anything down. It was only some years after his death that early Christians compiled the four different versions of his life and teachings that we call the Gospels.)

3.3 Problems of using translations

There cannot be any one accurate translation of the Bible. Each translator continually faces multiple choices between different manuscript versions and between different traditions for interpreting the words found in each version. And on top of this, they have their own convictions about what they and their branch of the Church want the Bible to be seen to say.

3.3.1 Sex and sexuality raise special difficulties for the translators. The Greeks had words for certain specific sex-acts, but they had no words that meant anything like 'homosexual' or 'homosexuality'. Nor does Hebrew have any such words. Whenever we see a word like 'homosexual' in an English Bible, we know that it simply cannot be there in the original. Some translator is adding a private spin.

All the different peoples living around the Mediterranean at this time—Jewish, Greek, Roman and others—were familiar with same-sex sexual activity. None of these civilisations felt that it implied some kind of non-standard 'homosexual' mind-set, or was a special inclination peculiar to a separate minority of their citizens. This whole idea is modern, dating from the 1850s. Our ancestors would have found it rather strange.

NOTES

1   For more general information see the appendix, A Note On Using The Bible.

2   For instance, some early copyist inserted twenty-five words into 1 John 5:7-8 in an attempt to influence doctrinal debates about the Trinity. This forgery is so blatant that it was eventually detected; however, you will still find this passage in some translations, more than three centuries after it was first exposed.

Another example: the text of Matthew 19:9 became corrupt at a very early stage in the church's history. Jesus's early followers rewrote this passage so thoroughly, and so variously, that Jesus's teaching on the subject of divorce and remarriage can never be recovered.

4   THE OLD TESTAMENT

The Old Testament contains much that is important to Christian doctrine, much that is of obscure significance, or which became extinct with the promulgation of the Gospel, and a certain amount of material that is deeply unedifying: one thinks immediately of the sexual irregularities of the great patriarchs, of the fraud by which Jacob stole his brother's inheritance, of Lot's daughters' rape of their own father, and of the appalling story of the laughing children who were torn apart by bears. (The prophet Elisha prayed for revenge on the children who had poked fun at his bald head. God listened, and sent the bears. *2 Kings 2:23-25*)

Most Christians read the Old Testament with careful discrimination. Some passages clearly might have doctrinal significance; others, even more clearly, do not; the rest have been under debate for two thousand years, and there is still no consensus.

4.1   The story of Adam and Eve

The biblical story of the creation of humankind exists in two different versions, written at different times. Whoever compiled the book we now call Genesis incorporated them both into the Creation-story, one after the other. In the first version *[Genesis 1:26-30]* God creates 'man' as a species, then tells 'them' to 'be fruitful and multiply, and replenish the earth'. There is no mention of Eden, of the two Trees, of the primal sin of disobedience, nor of God cursing humankind. No individuals of the new race are named, because there is no suggestion that he began by making only two people. In this version he created a whole species.

In the second, longer, version of the story *[Genesis 2:7 to 5:5]*, God creates just two people, who are named as Adam and Eve. This version of the story is concerned with (a) Adam's loneliness, in response to which God creates Eve to be his companion, and (b) their joint disobedience in eating the fruit of the tree of the knowledge of good and evil, and the terrible consequences of this act. There is no command that they 'be fruitful and multiply', which is hardly surprising: this version of the myth is not about how we came to exist, but about the ancient loss of a legendary Paradise. If this version had had anything to do with 'replenishing the earth' with humans, the writers would have had also to address the difficulty that if they were ever to have grandchildren, Adam and Eve would have had to marry their own daughters and sons off to each other—a peculiar example of large-scale incest. It is always unwise to press these mythological tales further than the original story-tellers intended, or in a different direction. Doctrinal authority cannot just be switched on and off like a tap.

When asked, "Do these chapters of Genesis, the Adam and Eve stories, have any power at all of being significant for Christian moral doctrine?", there are many Christians who would simply say "No". Like other parts of the Old

Testament, these ancient myths have no clear doctrinal authority within the Church.

But there are some homophobes who nevertheless try to argue from one or both of these stories that in some way the Creator 'wired' procreation and heterosexuality into the very fabric of his new world. They claim that homosexuals are therefore challenged by having a lesser, dysfunctional, sexuality. Let us look more closely at this.

4.1.1 Gay people, for thousands of years, have lived lives that demonstrate that the idea that our sexuality is either lesser than other people's, or dysfunctional, is not only wrong but bizarre. That could be seen as being the end of the matter; but it also has to be said that the theology of this argument is very seriously questionable. Many Christians reject this whole interpretation on the grounds that as a use of the Old Testament it is strained and doctrinally unsafe.

Even supported by the most favourable (that is, by the homophobes' own) interpretations of the New Testament, it is a strikingly large conclusion, resting precariously on a very small tip of evidence. When one discounts the single words in 1 Corinthians and 1 Timothy (as I think, in the end, one has to: see **5.3** below) this massive doctrine finds itself hanging by just one apostolic thread, Romans 1. In the face of the silence not only of Jesus, but of the whole of the rest of the New Testament, can Romans 1 be enough to uphold, or bring into flower a comprehensive, elaborate doctrine of human nature, with the most far-reaching consequences for all human life, whose only seed is an *ad hoc*, specially-motivated reading of this passage in Genesis? As we shall see below (**5.1**), the answer has to be 'no'.

4.1.3 In the first version mankind is told to 'be fruitful and multiply'. But here God is addressing the entire human species, not individuals—and undeniably, the species as a whole does do exactly this. We are perfectly capable of multiplying our numbers unhindered by the fact that a very large proportion of human sexual activity is and always has been non-procreative. Homosexuality is a part of the creation, and does not stand in the way of the fulfilment of God's command to the human species.

Some anti-gay writers give the unfortunate impression that they wish to blur the text here, by suggesting that in the 'be fruitful and multiply' version God was addressing one man and one woman. This is not the case, as even a brief look at the Bible will show.

4.1.4 The words 'he created them male and female' in the first version do *not* imply that the species is 'sexually bipolar'—that every individual is either purely male or purely female. No way. In both the Hebrew and the Greek versions it's clear that to be created in God's image is to participate in both sexes. God is one; and we are told that to create humankind male and female was to create them in his own, unified, image. Each individual member of the species is defined as participating in both male and female.

If we look around us, history, psychology, social life and biology all confirm this. There are, and there always have been, people who are homosexual by nature, people who are born physically hermaphrodite or intersexual, and people who are transgendered. The Genesis texts, read with exactness, scrupulously leave space for all the rich and difficult complexities of gender and sexuality that we have lived with ever since we became human.

If we can ever derive doctrine from any purely mythological passage in the Old Testament, it seems that we can conclude here that procreation is a function of the entire human species, but *not* of any one specific individual; and that the human race was *not* created to be 'sexually bipolar'. Rather, Genesis suggests that a human who was exclusively, or obsessively, either male or female in every respect would be, doctrinally speaking, a maimed creature, if s/he could exist at all under the created dispensation.

Many (heterosexual and other) Christians of various traditions would say just this. Others most certainly would not. But I repeat: reading the Old Testament, we are all haunted by the laughing children, and by Jacob's fraud. None of these stories has the clear doctrinal authority that could give any bigot—of any persuasion—the power to demand that anyone has to accept a particular reading as a matter of faith or dogma.

4.1.5 If the words 'be fruitful and multiply' had any doctrinal significance at all, they would not apply to homosexuality alone. People who are sterile or infertile would be condemned on exactly the same lines. Deliberately to choose celibacy or virginity would be a sin. 'White marriage' (a kind of Christian marriage where the couple abstains from all sexual intercourse) would be a perversion. It is easy to see that such a doctrine would be a great moral evil. The very idea looks on the page so strained as to be absurd. But that absurdity is the touchstone: between homosexuality and these other kinds of infertility there can be no moral distinction that is not absurd. Some are unable to 'be fruitful and multiply' because they are homosexual, some because their bodies produce no viable sperm, and others through a legitimate act of choice or self-definition. The condition, its source in nature, and the consequences, are all identical. So is its moral and doctrinal status.

In fact, the churches find themselves in a genuinely difficult position. They not only permit, or even encourage, celibacy and virginity, they freely celebrate heterosexual marriages between infertile couples—marriages where the male partner is sterile, or has undergone a surgical orchiectomy (castration), e.g. for cancer, or where the female partner has undergone a hysterectomy, or is many decades past the change of life. The Church sees, quite rightly, that marrying these couples raises no moral question at all; and yet against those who are infertile for equally good reasons, their sexuality, some modern Christians—not all—suddenly rush to man the barricades.

4.2   The story of Sodom and Gomorrah

This *[Genesis 19]* **is a story about a crime against hospitality, mistreating the strangers within the gates.** If it has doctrinal significance at all, then far from supporting the homophobes, it's something of a moral lesson directed *at* them.

4.2.1   The idea that this story was directed against general excess and self-indulgence (including promiscuity) is a misunderstanding which sprang up in late Jewish legends, and from here the idea was picked up by some in the early Church. New Testament writers associate the story with sexual promiscuity, but not with same-sex activity (see **5.7** below). Some later Christian homophobes redirected it again, aiming the story specifically against same-sex promiscuity. But the original point of the story is the abuse of hospitality.[1]

4.3   The Ten Commandments

Like the Adam and Eve story, the code we call the Ten Commandments exists in two different versions *[Exodus 20:1-17, Deuteronomy 5:6-21]*. Many Christians and others regard this code as a universal basis for human morality. It states that it is wrong to kill, to steal, to perjure oneself, to commit adultery, to blaspheme, to be envious, &c... **but the Ten Commandments say nothing at all about sexuality.**

The Ten Commandments have a unique status, both in the Bible and in the Judaeo-Christian tradition of moral thought. They are the foundation and the epitome of the Christian moral law. It is of the greatest significance that this impressive code, graven in stone, shows no concern about homosexuality at all.

4.4   Leviticus: "abomination" and local taboo

Early Israelite law-makers said at Leviticus 18:22 (repeated at Leviticus 20:13) that it is in Hebrew '*to`evah*' for an Israelite man to 'sleep the sleep of a woman with a man'.

4.4.1   We shall come back to the phrase 'sleep the sleep of a woman with a man'. What about the Hebrew word *to`evah*? The King James Version and Douay-Rheims translators said it meant 'abomination'. So did the translators of the New English Bible and the Revised English Bible, though they ought to have known better. The Jerusalem Bible translators wrote 'a hateful thing', which their less bigoted revisors might have corrected in the New Jerusalem Bible, but did not.

It means nothing like any of these. *To`evah* is a precise, limited word meaning 'taboo'. As used throughout the five Books of the Law, it has no general moral significance at all. The rules about *to`evah* only ever applied to Israelites living in Palestine, and the practices they referred to have been extinct for over two thousand years. For these verses refer exclusively to a particular sexual religious ceremony practised by the Canaanite neighbours of the early Israelites, a ceremony that involved a man worshipping the earth-goddess by having sex with the male prostitutes consecrated to her service in her temples. These two verses, like all the other to'evah rules in the Pentateuch, are as dead as Tiglath-Pileser: the Canaanite temples have crumbled to archaeological ruins, and the Canaanite religions are long extinct. Even in St Paul's day, only a few centuries later, these verses of Leviticus were defunct. Paul himself never referred to them, not even in Romans 1 (see **5.1** below). Nor did any other New Testament writer.[2]

4.4.2   The phrase 'sleep the sleep of a woman with a man' seems to mean quite specifically, in both the Hebrew and the Greek versions, 'to be penetrated by another man'. But homophobic translators are noticeably reluctant to be accurate about this; they broaden the phrase out so as to include as much same-sex activity as they think they can get away with. The people responsible for the version called the Good News Bible actually wrote here 'have sexual relations with another man'—which is not a translation, but a perversion of the text.

4.4.3   We must note that the word to'evah has no moral significance at all. It does not refer to any absolute ideas of Good and Evil. Old Testament usage makes it clear that to'evah was local, and relative to the local culture, whatever that was. While they were living in Egypt, the Israelites freely altered their own behaviour so as not to offend the Egyptians' quite different rules of to'evah, however alien or bizarre these rules seemed to the Israelites *[Genesis 43:32, 46:34, Exodus 8:26]*. Translators often fail to make it clear (or avoid making it clear) that each of these interesting and important verses centres on the same word that is used about male-male sex-rituals in Leviticus.

Modern translators are intriguingly inconsistent about this word. In the context of sacred idols or phallic poles they translate it simply as 'idol' or 'idolatry'. *[Deut 7:25 (GNB), 7:26 (NEB), 32:16 (NIV), 2 Chr 34:33 (NIV, REB revising NEB]*. But in the passages where we see the Jews conforming to the Egyptians' local taboos, they dilute the Egyptian taboo to 'they considered it beneath their dignity' [GNB, *Gen 43:32]*, or 'shepherds are regarded as unclean by the Egyptians' [REB, *Gen 46:34]*, It's only in the context of same-sex sex that the translators reach for melodramatic terms of abuse like 'disgusting practice' or 'abomination'! Yet it's all the same word in Hebrew.

4.4.4   Ancient Hebrew did have words for calling certain acts morally wrong, but in the whole of the Bible these words are *never* used of same-sex sex. For instance, it is *tevel*, 'a violation of the natural order', for a woman to have sex with an animal *[Lev 18:23]*. Brother-sister incest *[Lev 20:17]* is *hesed*: something socially scandalous. Downright sexual immorality, such as pimping for one's own daughter *[Lev 19:29]* is *zimah*. But *nowhere* in the Bible is it suggested that any of these words apply to same-sex sex. And conversely, nowhere in the Bible is the word to'evah, 'taboo', ever used of any such behaviour.[3]

4.4.5 Some of the rules in Leviticus 18-20 echo principles that we can all happily agree with, such as being courteous to old people and hospitable to visitors *[Lev 19:32-34]*. Other rules are universally agreed to be dead, except for certain strict orthodox Jews: for instance, the bans on cross-breeding cattle and wearing mixed fabrics such as polyester-and-cotton *[Lev 19:19]*, or on sowing and harvesting crops in the seventh year (see **3.1** above). Again: there are reasons why men and women tend to avoid sex during the woman's period, but obedience to the laws of ritual purity in Leviticus is not one of them. Not even the strictest Christian would suggest that men and women who do do this must be expelled from the United Kingdom *[Lev 20:18]*.

It is fair to ask those who cite Leviticus 18:22 and 20:13 against gay Christians to explain why they think these rules about Canaanite rituals of worship somehow have force against their own Christian neighbours, when their own lives demonstrate that other, equally stern rules of behaviour laid down in the Pentateuch are dead letters.

4.5   The crime at Gibeah

This *[Judges 19-21]* is a story of the extermination of the tribe of Benjamin by the other Israelite tribes. The war began because the Benjaminites had betrayed their duties of hospitality towards a visitor. The story is openly modelled on the legend in Genesis about the similar abuse of hospitality at Sodom. Reading all three chapters, it is clear that in the visitor's eyes the breach of hospitality began and ended with the gang-rape and death of his female concubine. The idea that the townsmen originally wanted to have sex with him is simply not part of his cause of complaint. The story confirms that the taboo in Leviticus was aimed only against sex-worship of Canaanite gods.

4.6   The word "sodomite"

Some English translations use the word "sodomite" in parts of the Old Testament we have not yet looked at. The Hebrew original in these places is either a word that means "someone living in the town of Sodom" (just as "Londoner" means "someone living in London"), or else a quite different root that means "consecrated" or "holy", and thus a temple prostitute.

4.6.1 Wisdom 19:13-17. The topic here is again the proper treatment of visiting strangers (see **4.2** and **4.5** above). The writer declares that the Egyptians offended against the laws of hospitality far more dreadfully than did the townspeople of Sodom, for the Egyptians enslaved their visiting strangers, while the people of Sodom merely tried to get theirs to have sex with them. (Hardly a comforting passage for the puritans, come to think of it.)[4]

4.6.2 Elsewhere *[e.g. KJV: Deut 23:17, 1 Kings 14:24, 15:12, 22:46, 2 Kings 23:7]*, the word "sodomite" is a false translation. The Hebrew word here has nothing to do with the inhabitants of Sodom, nor with same-sex sexual behaviour. The word is *qadash*, "consecrated male prostitute". (See **4.4.1** above.)

NOTES

1 For a very similar story, making exactly the same point, see **4.5** below. See also **4.6.1** and **5.7**. All our Mediterranean ancestors were very concerned with the responsibilities of hosts and guests. The plot of Homer's *Odyssey,* for example, centres on the hospitality-trap: there is simply no socially acceptable way for Telemachus and his mother to get rid of guests who refuse to leave. Like the earliest books of the Old Testament, the *Odyssey* dates from the 8th century B.C.

2   In practice the taboo was impossible to enforce. As recent British history shows all too bleakly, legislation does not abolish same-sex love or sex: you can only legislate to punish your victims afterwards, if they are found out. Not even the most terrible penalties act as a deterrent. In spite of Leviticus, even the Kings of Israel and Judah adopted Canaanite worship and set up special houses for the sacred male prostitutes, which their reforming successor, Josiah, pulled down when he came to the throne *[2 Kings 23:7].* Lower down in society, we see *[Deut 23:17-18]* that Israelites not only picked up beer-money as sacred prostitutes in the rival establishment, they even used these earnings (cheekily or blasphemously, depending on your point of view) to pay for their offerings in the Temple of Jehovah.

3   Unfortunately these important distinctions are invisible to English readers: the translators blur all these words together. When we see an English word like 'abomination', 'wickedness', 'detestable practice', &c., it is impossible to tell whether it is here translating *tumah* or *sheqets,* 'ritual uncleanness', or *to`evah* or *pigul,* 'a tainted offering', or any of the others. The reader can only find out by consulting the Hebrew.

4   You may not be able to find the book of Wisdom in the version you are using: it's one of the bits that some churches leave out of the Bible altogether.

5 THE NEW TESTAMENT

As we saw in section **2**, Jesus himself saw nothing to criticise in same-sex inclinations or activities. We turn to the pastoral letters of his apostle, Paul.

5.1 Romans 1:13-32

The Christian converts in Rome had a mixed background: some had been converted from Judaism, others from paganism (the Roman and Greek state religion). Paul had been told that these two backgrounds were not melding well with each other in the little new Church: that is why he sat down and dictated this letter. He was a powerful and able administrator, driven by his passion for uniformity and harmony within the organisation, but he had not yet been able to visit Rome to assess the situation for himself, and address the sectarian issues there. Both Jews and pagans had carried on enjoying a lot of the religious and social practices that were part of their two different cultural heritages, in spite of the fact that in Christian eyes these things were idolatrous or otherwise unsound—and the Christian church in Rome was turning into what appears to have been a bizarre eclectic mixture of old Jewish, old pagan and new Christian social rituals and religious observances.

Paul was deeply disturbed by what he had heard. In this letter he set out to lay down rules that would cut off Christian Romans once and for all from the other two cultures: an extremely hard task, considering that both Judaism and paganism were omnipresent in these people's day-to-day lives. Paul is in fact writing rules of separateness intended to reinforce the identity of a dissident minority surrounded by an attractive mass culture—a very local and specific task. The writers of Leviticus had done exactly the same a few centuries earlier when they wrote taboos forbidding Israelites to share in the social and religious lifestyles of their Canaanite neighbours. (See **4.4** above.)

5.1.1 He begins by trying to diminish the appeal of paganism in his readers' eyes. (It has to be said that this was an uphill task: paganism, like the old Canaanite religions, had a good deal about it that people might well find attractive). He abuses the pagans for believing in the wrong gods, studying philosophy, and enjoying sex *'para physin'*, which means 'more than', or 'beyond', what is 'natural'. (Translators like to render it more dramatically as *'against* nature', but this is misleading.) Women do it in some way he doesn't specify, and men do it with each other. Not only that, the pagans are greedy, break promises, spread gossip, and have been known to be disobedient to their parents. Clearly, in Paul's eyes, people who believe in the wrong God, behave the wrong way. But is this relevant to us, now? If we are not Christians, then the answer must be—no, not at all. We do not need St Paul to tell us that murder and ingratitude are morally wrong, and we do not accept that he has any right to add sexuality, or even gossip, to the list.

5.1.2 Paul's concern in Romans 1 is not the nature of sexuality, nor the structure of the family, nor even sexual morality, but something quite different from all these: the attitude of new converts towards the familiar pagan heritage that surrounded them. His specifics—ingratitude to parents, sexual behaviour, gossip, greed &c.—are illustrations of his argument, not its subject.

5.1.3   The passage itself is not perfectly clear. If he's saying that same-sex activity is on the same moral level as gossip, it's difficult to see why the homophobes think this passage serves their cause. If, however, he's saying *[Rom 1:30-32]* that not only homosexuals, but also everyone who is envious, or arrogant, or slanderous, all those who distort the truth or who disobey their parents, and those who are simply *stupid*, all actually deserve to die... then surely this is not Christian doctrine at all, and never has been?

There are indeed Christians in whose eyes this passage in Romans 1 appears to have no significance at all, except as raw material for constructing a weapon against gays.

> Note Paul's word *asunetoi*, 'the stupid': literally in Greek it means 'slow on the uptake'. Did Paul really intend to stigmatise learning disability as a moral fault? The text is clear: he did. But do the homophobes follow Paul that far? They do not. They choose the words that please them, and disregard the rest.

5.1.4   Basically, in Paul's eyes, the old pagan worship seems to have involved people in doing things that were somehow against their own individual nature. This may have made sense for him, in some contemporary context now obscure to us, but it has no application to homosexuals now. For there is no question: it is *by nature* that we are gay. Even the Roman Catholic Church, under this present, very conservative, Pope, has now officially declared that it is indeed *natural*, not 'beyond' nature, for people to be homosexual, and that what Paul wrote in Romans 1 has to be interpreted in this light.

In fact the obvious and natural thought is that for us, 'perversion' would be to try to bend ourselves against the grain into heterosexual behaviour, or to bully or scare ourselves into an unnatural and destructive celibacy.[1]

5.1.5   As we saw above, Paul has the same general purpose as the writers of Leviticus. He also has the same specific subject: idolatry. Like the writers of Leviticus 18-20, he is talking about male-male sex in the special context of worshipping pagan gods via sacred images—men, birds, animals and reptiles *[Rom 1:23-28]*. The original taboos against Canaanite rituals were extinct, of course, like the Canaanite religion itself (note again that Paul never referred, here or elsewhere, to those two dead verses in Leviticus); but there were other popular orgiastic religions with sacred sex in Paul's world, such as the cult of the goddess Cybele.

5.1.6   In Paul's reference to women doing something that's wrong *[Rom 1:26]*, we may, if we wish, see a reference to lesbianism. However, the early Church Fathers did not. Indeed the syntax of the Greek suggests that when Paul explains, later in the sentence, that what men do wrong is 'doing shameless things with men' (i.e. using sacred prostitutes for ritual sex), he does so precisely because this is *not* parallel with whatever the women do. It is possible that Paul is referring to women who perform non-procreative intercourse. Many in the early Church (and more recently too!) regarded the 'natural use' of women as exclusively that of being child-breeders, or 'living incubators'. (See **6.2.3** below). But it must be said that the Greek is imprecise and obscure. He might have had lesbianism somewhere in his mind, or he might not. We cannot tell. Nor can the Church erect a doctrine on a guess.

5.1.7 Paul's attitude to sex is consistently wary, or ascetic—many Christians would say puritanical. His attitudes towards both prostitution and idolatry are ferociously negative; and when these last combine, as perhaps they do here, one would expect stern language and strong feeling.

While doing justice by Paul's passion for the moral values of integrity and fidelity, the Church has always been prepared to read his pronouncements on sex with interpretative care. He was, after all, convinced that the second coming of the risen Christ and the end of the world were so close upon the new Church that the procreation of a new generation, indeed all sexual activity, must be quite irrelevant, and therefore self-indulgent. And Paul, personally, had no time for anything that looked to him like self-indulgence. How far anyone agrees with Paul's personal definition of what is and what is not self-indulgence is of course entirely a matter of individual judgement.

5.1.8 Some of what Paul wrote has been reassessed by the Church as the world has changed—not only the sexual asceticism. He explicitly condones slavery—several times *[Ephes 6:5-6, Coloss 3:22-4:1, 1 Tim 6:1-2, Titus 2:9-10]* and he refuses women their request for an equal part in Christian worship, declaring that women have a lower moral status than men—and they must never wear jewellery, or plait their hair. *[1 Corinth 11:2-16, Ephes 5:22-28, Coloss 3:18, 1 Tim 2:9-15.]* He permits lay members of the Church (though not deacons or church elders) to have more than one wife or concubine. *[1 Tim 3:1-7,8-14, Titus 1:5-9].*[2] These passages have long been consigned to the history-books—why not this one too? It's not as if Paul marked the statements about slaves and women with some kind of 'sell-by' date. The mind-set that he wished to eradicate from his difficult new converts in Rome, a nostalgia for the familiar habits and rituals of their pagan upbringing, is long extinct.

5.2   How not to translate Romans I

Read the whole Letter to the Romans yourself, if you are concerned. Make up your own mind. But problems of translation are even more significant in the New Testament than in the Old. For example:

5.2.1 Those words 'beyond what is natural' (*para physin*) are exactly the phrase that Paul uses at Romans 11:24 of the working of God's Holy Spirit in the world. Whatever he meant by 'natural', the phrase is evidently not loaded with negative connotations in his mind.

18

5.2.2 Some older English versions *[KJV, DR, RSV]* translate '*tēs planēs autōn*' in verse 27 as 'their error'. This is quite accurate: *planē*, 'error', is not a strongly negative word. Modern English versions, however *[NEB, REB, JB, NJB, NIV]* like to translate it as 'their perversion', which is spicier, but not what Paul wrote.

It is interesting that when Paul uses this word *planē*, 'error', in contexts that have nothing to do with sex, the same translators unemotively render it as 'delusion' or even, with an unintended irony, 'misleading'.[3]

5.2.3 You will find at Rom 1:27 that all the translators use a phrase that reads something like 'received in themselves the due penalty for their perversion' *[NIV]*. For 'perversion' see above; but note also that the idea of penalty or punishment is being added by the translators. Paul merely indicates that these people charged a fee for their services, as prostitutes always have done, whether consecrated or not.[4]

5.3   1 Corinthians and 1 Timothy

Two other passages in Paul's letters, 1 Corinthians 6:9 and 1 Timothy 1:10, are sometimes cited. Like Romans 1:29-32, these passages are lists of kinds of people of whom Paul more or less strongly disapproves.

> Paul gives other such lists at (e.g.) 1 Cor 5:11, 2 Cor 12:10-11, Gal 5:19-20, Ephes 5:3-5, Coloss 3:5-8, and 2 Tim 3:2-9. Not one of these contains any word that could possibly be applied to any question of sexual orientation.

5.3.1 In 1 Corinthians 6:9 Paul begins his list with fornicators, idolaters, and adulterers. The next word occurs elsewhere in the New Testament meaning either 'people who are physically ill' *[Matt 4:23, 9:35, 10:1]* or 'people who are well-dressed' *[Matt 11:8, Luke 7:25]*. You can see there is a certain amount of fog around—but it still takes a good deal of imagination to declare that when Paul uses this word here it has something to do with gay sex. But this is exactly what some translators do. In 1 Cor 6:9 they suddenly start translating it as if it meant 'the effeminate' *[KJV, DR]*, or 'male prostitutes' *[NIV]*, or 'catamites' *[JB]*.

> The root meaning of this common Greek word, *malakos*, is 'gentle', 'peaceful' or 'unruffled by anger'. By New Testament times it had come to be used very much as we use our own word 'weak': that is, either 'physically ill', or 'psychologically easy-going' (hence unself-critical, hence self-indulgent, hence expensively-dressed). Those who declare that, for Paul, 'weak' and 'over-dressed' *must* have added up to 'effeminate', are adorning their own fantasies with anachronistic stereotypes derived from Liberace.

The word has in fact nothing at all to do with sexuality. All credit to the revisors who have altered 'catamites' *[JB, 1968]* to 'the self-indulgent' *[NJB, 1985]*: an accurate translation, unbiased by homophobia.

More credit at Gal 5:19, where the same revisors have corrected 'gross indecency' (which in legal and tabloid English refers to a male-male sexual crime) to the accurate and neutral word 'impurity'.

5.3.2 The word that follows this in 1 Corinthians 6:9 is a far more serious problem, for all the translators. It turns up again in another of Paul's lists (1 Timothy 1:10). In these two places they choose to make Paul denounce 'homosexuals', 'sodomites', 'perverts' (even 'child-molesters'—that was Luther's guess, and quite impossible—see **5.6** below). But the fact is... it's all fiction. Even the basic meaning of this word has been lost for nearly two thousand years. It is found nowhere else in the Bible, nor in any earlier Greek literature that survives. As far as we know Paul was the first, and the last in his own epoch, to use it. Its dictionary meaning is unknown (and has therefore been filled in by guesswork). It certainly seems to contain a Greek root meaning 'fuck', and therefore to have something to do with sex; but specifically homosex? No. It could be anything.[5]

5.3.3 There were many established words and phrases in contemporary Greek that denoted various male-male sex acts (e.g. *kinaideia, arrenomixia, paiderastia*). But in all his various lists of malefactors, scattered throughout his pastoral letters, Paul uses none of them: not one.

5.3.4 After Paul's death we can find some Christian writers who were in some sense anti-gay, and who said so clearly—far more clearly than any passage that anyone can find in the Bible. These writers have no special authority in matters of doctrine: their views are simply personal. But they did speak the same dialect of Greek as Paul, and presumably shared an understanding of what this mystery word meant—and it is a very important fact that not one of these bigots ever seized on either of these verses from 1 Corinthians or 1 Timothy for use against gays, not even in passages where they are openly ransacking the entire Bible for texts that might support their prejudice.

5.3.5 Those few writers who did use this word, a century or so after Paul's death, don't use it in the context of same-sex sex. Either they simply put it in a list, or quote it directly from Paul, thus giving us no clues as to what it actually meant either to Paul or to themselves,[6] or else they used it in contexts where it clearly means something quite different: women who use anal sex as a contraceptive measure, for example (some early Church fathers seem to have hated contraception, though this is another subject neither Jesus nor Paul ever thought of mentioning), or free-born citizens who demean themselves by acting as prostitutes.[7] It is not possible to tell whether either of these was the basic meaning the word had earlier had for Paul.

5.3.6 Many Christians believe that whatever this word meant to Paul, there is a legible message in the fact that the Holy Spirit working in history has seen fit to let its meaning fade, blur, and die.

5.4   General problems of translating lists

The very structure of these lists, a string of nouns placed side-by-side, makes them all peculiarly difficult to translate. No noun has a context that might illuminate the sense in which Paul was using it. In lists like this we bump our noses painfully against the fact of how very little we really know about the day-to-day usage of this dialect of Greek amongst Paul's audience.

5.4.1   For example, some translators say that the Greek word *pleonektai* means 'the greedy', others 'the promiscuous', and others again 'usurers', or 'the avaricious'. (The JB translators hedge their bets, putting 'usurers' at 1 Cor 6:9, 'promiscuity' at Ephes 5:5, and then 'greed' at Coloss 3:5.) No-one knows what this word actually meant to Paul.

5.4.2   Again, it is difficult to guess what difference Paul might have seen between *eris, zēlos, akatastasia, eritheia, echthrai and hairēsis*, which all mean something like 'strife', 'jealousies', 'dissension' or 'factiousness'.

5.4.3   Yet again, the words *akatharsia, aselgeia, aischrotes* and *porneia* (or *pornos*) all find themselves translated along the lines of 'impurity', 'uncleanness', 'licentiousness', 'debauchery', 'immorality', 'whoremonger', 'fornicator' &c. In modern English these are simply vague terms of abuse. People apply them to suit their own prejudices and preferences. If Paul, and the people he was writing to, made any useful distinction of meaning here, it is long lost to us.

5.4.4   In some of Paul's lists we find the translations vary confusingly, because there are problems with the Greek text. For instance, at Rom 1:29, Rom 1:31, Gal 5:19 and Gal 5:21 the manuscripts disagree about whether or not Paul included 'murderers', 'truce-breakers' (or should this word perhaps be 'the implacable'?), 'fornicators', or 'adulterers'. Different translators have included different words. (There is a very similar textual problem at Mark 7:22. This affects words attributed to Jesus himself.)

5.5   Paul on moral integrity

By contrast, Paul states his disapproval of promiscuity quite clearly. There is no question here: Paul says that the Church can demand that its members all live their lives under certain rules of fidelity. But the homophobes cannot claim that there is Pauline authority for demanding that homosexuals lead lesser lives than others.

Integrity, for Paul, did not end with sex, or even, perhaps, centre on it. There is intellectual integrity as well. It is interesting to remember that when the Latin root 'pervert-' (from which we derived the English word 'perversion') first appears in a translation of a Bible, the translator St Jerome applied it to *giving false judgement*. For Jerome, 'perversion' meant intellectual dishonesty, not sexual misconduct.[8]

5.6   How not to translate 1 Timothy 1:10

Before passing on, let us look at one very interesting point about the mystery word in 1 Timothy 1:10. Here, one particular translation demonstrates quite disturbingly how very vulnerable readers of the Bible are to the invisible manipulations of the translators. In the Jerusalem Bible version (published in 1968) this passage read "for murderers, for *those who are immoral with women or with boys or with men*, for liars...". *[JB, 1968]*

But in the revised New Jerusalem Bible (1985) the same passage runs "for murderers, *for the promiscuous, homosexuals, kidnappers*, for liars..." *[NJB, 1985]*.

The murderers and the liars are the same, and we also recognise that 'homosexuals' replaces 'those who are immoral with men', while 'the promiscuous' are presumably 'those who are immoral with women'. But where have the child-molesters gone, 'those who are immoral with boys'? Even more mysterious, where have these 'kidnappers' come from? It's difficult to imagine that both versions are translating the same Greek words.

But they are. This is not a question of variant manuscript-readings.

What happened, apparently, was this. The 1968 translators decided that they would improve on Luther's unpleasant fantasy about child-molesters, and pretend that in this verse the mystery word definitely meant 'men who have sex with boys'. (It definitely doesn't. The word contains no root that could possibly relate to young people or children—of either sex.) They then decided to translate 'the promiscuous' as 'men who are immoral with women', which makes sense. But unfortunately—in the translators' eyes—this left gays in the clear: after all, we are not promiscuous with women, and we are not child-molesters. This was not what they wished the Bible to be seen to say. So it appears that they deliberately mistranslated the word 'kidnappers' as 'men who are immoral with men'.[9]

Seventeen years later the revisors, perhaps a little ashamed of their predecessors, quietly put back the kidnappers and abandoned the impossible 'child-molesters', replacing them with 'homosexuals'. Still wrong, still bigoted, still anachronistic, and still guesswork—but they have at least done a kind of justice to kidnappers.

5.7   Jude 1:3-10 and 2 Peter 2:6-10

Both these passages refer to the town of Sodom, but there is no hint here of same-sex acts. The Jewish legend these authors have in mind said that the *women* of Sodom had intercourse with the 'strange flesh' of the angels. The legend itself is a misunderstanding of the original story: see **4.2** above.

5.8   The word "dogs"

The word 'dogs', *kunes*, in two places in the New Testament is sometimes said to be a contemporary slang word that meant either 'male prostitutes' or 'catamites'.

5.8.1 At Philippians 3:2 this is obviously not the case. Paul is warning his listeners against preachers of false doctrine who have managed to gain people's ears within the Church; in particular, against members of a conservative fundamentalist pressure-group who were teaching that new converts to Christianity had to go through the Jewish rite of physical circumcision. "Dogs in the church" would have seemed a very apt metaphor for people who have sneaked in to the Church and are fouling the place up with false doctrine.[10]

5.8.2 At Revelation 22:15 John writes that "dogs, fortune-tellers, and fornicators, and murderers, and idolaters and everyone of false speech and false life" *[JB]* are barred from heaven. It is possible that John had Temple prostitutes in mind—we can also see idolaters in the list, after all, and we tend to find them together. But in view of the concluding words 'false speech and false life', it seems likely that 'dogs' meant the same to John as it did to Paul: sectarian teachers of false doctrine within the Church.

NOTES

1   The renunciatory or sacrificial celibacy that this particular group of homophobes preach is not Christian celibacy at all, but the reviled (and heretical) Catharist practice of *endura*: 'purifying' one's self by an extended act of self-destruction. "Indeed Heresies perish not with their Authors, but like the river *Arethusa*, though they lose their currents in one place, they rise up againe in another." (Sir Thomas Browne)

2   Some translators attempt to salvage these passages by rewriting them, but the Greek is clear: when choosing an elder from amongst the congregation, he ought to be 'the husband of one woman'. At 1 Tim 3:12 Paul shows that his concern is for domestic peace and quiet: elders must not be distracted from Church duties by warring factions amongst their womenfolk at home.

3   E.g. Gal 6:7, 1 Thess 2:3 'delude'; Titus 3:3 'misled'; JB.

4   Compare 2 Cor 6:13, the only other place where Paul uses the word '*antimisthia*'.

5   With impenetrable reasoning, the RSV translators stir both these two words together at 1 Cor 6:9 and come up with 'homosexuals' (see their footnote), though at 1 Tim 1:10, where the mystery word stands alone, they take a deep breath and say 'sodomite'.

6   Polycarp, *Philippians* 5; Theophilus *Ad Autolycum* 1:2,14; Nilus, *Epist.* 2:282.

7   E.g. Eusebius, *Demonstratio evangelica* 1:6; Aristides, *Apologia* 13 (Greek version, = Syriac 9).

8   Some British people, like the British tabloid newspapers, assume that 'impurity', 'uncleanness', 'immorality', and so on, must always refer to some kind of *sexual* impurity. In fact, in New Testament Greek I think this is true of only one of these: *porneia*, though in later centuries *aselgeia* moved a little in this direction. I observe that some tend to interpret words like *pornos* as referring to whoever it is that they themselves are most inclined to hate or fear.

9   'Kidnappers', *andrapodistai*, is an ordinary unambiguous Greek word, widely documented. It has nothing to do with sex.

10 It used to be taboo to let a dog get inside a place of worship. In Orthodox churches it still is.

6   SEXUALITY AND THE CHURCH

In its early days, when it was closest in time to Jesus and his disciples, the Christian Church was not institutionally homophobic. There were puritans in the Church, of course, as there are in any human society—but they were not in control.

6.1   The Early Church

The early Church solemnised same-sex marriages on equal terms with mixed-sex marriages. This fact has been 'forgotten' for about three hundred years (not long in the life of a two-thousand-year-old Church); but it is now back in the light of day, bright and clear. Some of the original services have now been reprinted.[1]

These same-sex ceremonies invoked the blessings of pairs of male saints (including Jesus's disciples Philip and Bartholomew), and they omitted the mention of children. Otherwise they are parallel in form and substance to the heterosexual ceremonies. In the old service-books, they are placed one after the other.

6.2   Some Early Church writers

Some early Christian Fathers did write against certain same-sex sexual acts. Why? And how far does this matter?

6.2.1   The early Fathers of the Church have little authority. Some Christians will not allow them any authority at all. But there is no church or pressure-group that would dream of taking all their teachings at face value: what they wrote is always being re-evaluated in the context of what we know about their own culture, and in the light of the way the Church developed, and still continues to develop, to meet the challenges of a changing world.

For the Church does so develop—in various directions. For instance. The last recorded same-sex marriage solemnised by the Church in Western Europe was as recent as 1578, in St John's Church at the Latin Gate in Rome; but by then the slow-gathering wave of mediæval social homophobia had reached such a height that the participants were lynched afterwards by the secular Roman mob. In the face of such bigotry, the Western Church drew back from its old traditions, and began to accommodate itself to contemporary popular prejudice. Same-sex marriages continued to take place well into the nineteenth, and possibly the early twentieth century in isolated, traditionally-minded regions of (e.g.) Albania and Bulgaria—places that were slow to conform to this new, essentially suburban, prejudice.

6.2.2   The Church fathers' denunciations of same-sex sexual activity can be pulled out and looked at in small quotes—and they frequently are. Once replaced in their context, however, their effect is markedly diluted. It becomes apparent that these statements are part—neither a large nor a central part—of a general programme of physical puritanism, expressed in a violent distaste for all sexual activity. These authors wanted to use rhetoric, doctrinal argument, even internal Church politics, to build their personal distaste for sex into a formal ecclesiastical machine for controlling *all* aspects of human sexual behaviour. They failed.

6.3   Early Church Fathers and Women

One specific principle generated the homophobic rhetoric of these early Church Fathers: a passionate conviction that women are greatly inferior to men. Fuelled by this unpleasant prejudice, they denounced male-male anal sex as being a betrayal of the essential superiority of man over woman because, the way they looked at it, this seemed to reduce one of the men to having the status of a woman. John Chrysostom shows this sentiment with frankness—to our eyes, startling frankness—in his remarks on Romans 1. For instance, he argues *[Homily 4]* that though dogs are useful animals in themselves, a man would be rightly insulted by a suggestion that he might turn himself into a dog. Surely, therefore, a man must be utterly enraged by the thought of degrading himself so very far as to behave like a woman.

Few now would hesitate before rejecting this whole attitude. Chrysostom's contempt and loathing for pregnancy and childbirth are difficult to read without disgust. Yet it is this which generates his and his contemporaries' homophobia, blinding them even to the fact—perfectly well known in their day—that to reduce either love or sexuality to questions of anatomical mechanics is a surreal diminution of our lives.

6.3.1   However widely these men were admired for their pastoral and spiritual eloquence, in their own day, as I said above, they failed to influence either public opinion or Church policy towards the establishing of formal ecclesiastical control over sexual behaviour.

6.4   The High Middle Ages

It was not till more than seven hundred years after Chrysostom's death that the Church began moving towards an institutional control of marriage and sexuality, and hence towards institutional homophobia. Ironically, this takes us into the High Middle Ages, the most morally, doctrinally and politically corrupt period in the entire history of the Church. Most of these mediæval corruptions (including a virulent and murderous anti-semitism) have now been reformed out of the various branches of the Church. Most, not all. Homophobia is the one of the last, and perhaps the most persistent, still remaining.

6.4.1   Roman Catholics and some Anglicans declare that church doctrine is founded in 'the traditions of the Church' as well as in Scripture. They are referring to a very select slice through a history which could be called, at best, both rich and chequered. Read in one way, Church history can provide stronger authority for a vicious anti-semitism than for (say) priestly celibacy, or the sacramental status of marriage. It would not be intrinsically wrong for these churches to reassess their current line of sight through the past, and to abolish what was once a mediæval novelty. After all, they have done it before, in respect of slavery, polygamy, usury, and the shape of the solar system.

6.5   The evidence of history

The fact that the early Church celebrated same-sex marriages, and went on doing so for three-quarters of its existence to date, suggests that neither the Apostles nor their successors thought there was anything in the teaching of Jesus, or elsewhere in the Bible, that gave grounds for Christians to discriminate on grounds of sexuality.

NOTES

1   Professor J. Boswell, *Same Sex Unions in Pre-Modern Europe*, New York, 1994. I take the opportunity of recording that, even though I don't entirely agree with it, I am greatly indebted to Boswell's first learned and ground-breaking study, *Christianity, Social Tolerance and Homosexuality: Gay People in Western Europe from the Beginning of the Christian Era to the Fourteenth Century*, Chicago, 1980.

7   CONCLUSION

It is difficult to believe that this doctrine of discrimination, fear and self-doubt, so violent in its social effects, so intrinsically unjust, so destructive of the peace of mind of the innocent and vulnerable, and so much at variance with the spirit of the founder of Christianity, can have been woven out of such thin material as this.

For many, it will perhaps be the silences that speak loudest: the silence of the Moral Law, the Ten Commandments; and the silence of Jesus, who, for Christians, was and is incarnate God, the source and centre of the entire created world. I can understand that these two silences seem to many Christians, now and in the past, to harmonise into one vast and welcoming space, within which the created nature of gay and lesbian Christians can expand into that fullness of life which Jesus unforgettably promised all his followers.

Looking in the other direction, nothing in the great spiritual and theological cathedral that is the Christian Church is diminished by taking a broom to inhuman and destructive prejudice, or by clearing out barriers to that truth which (Jesus also promised) once learned, would make Christians free. So much has been done to rid the Church of the other corruptions that crept in during the High Middle Ages, and made nests for themselves in dark corners of the fabric, that it seems to many people—Christians and others—that the time for dealing with this last survival of cruelty and superstition has now arrived.

A NOTE ON USING THE BIBLE

The Christian Bible has come down to us in a mixture of Ancient Hebrew and Hellenistic Greek. Both these languages are now dead. Each of the many different books that you see on the shelf when you look for the Bible in a bookshop is an attempt made by someone to translate the original Hebrew and Greek text into a language still alive. In all cases the translation has been tailored to support the translators' private preferences, which are usually those of their own church, whatever it is. Oddly enough, very few of these translations contain a statement actually telling purchasers which particular church it was produced by. However they all claim, contradictorily, to be 'correct'.

The Bible is divided into two sections called the Old Testament and the New Testament. (Some versions also have a middle section called "The Apocrypha".)

The Old Testament and Apocrypha contain Jewish writings that date from before Jesus was born. The first five books in the Old Testament (Christians call them Genesis, Exodus, Leviticus, Numbers and Deuteronomy) are also known as the "Torah", or the "Pentateuch", or "the five Books of the Law".

The New Testament begins with four different versions of the life of Jesus called the four Gospels. Other books in the New Testament record the development of the new Church in the decades after Jesus's death.

Christians often call the Bible "the word of God" (but this means very different things for different groups). Some parts of it have a good deal of "authority" for some Christians. That means that they read these parts with intense care and respect, and try to derive "doctrine" and "theology" from them. (The word "doctrine" means, roughly, rules of moral behaviour that are based on a theory about the nature of God. "Theology" means "the science of studying God".) The four Gospels have most obvious authority, since they claim to record the deeds and words of Jesus himself. Other parts of the Bible (which parts? Well, it depends on what group of Christians you are listening to) have far less "authority" than the Gospels, or no authority at all. In general, New Testament books have more "authority" than Old Testament books.

Many Christians believe that the Early Church, being so close to Jesus, is the ideal all churches should follow. Unfortunately there is a lot we don't know about how the first Christians lived and taught, but we do know they had some practices that would be completely unacceptable nowadays. (Slavery, for instance. Also polygamy).

Each book in the Bible has a name, like "Genesis", or "Psalms", or "1 Corinthians". (This is short for "the first of the letters St Paul wrote to Christians living in the town of Corinth".) Most Bibles have a contents page at the front, which will tell you on which page to find each book. And each book is divided into chapters, and every chapter is divided into small bits called "verses", so we can refer to a few words anywhere in the Bible by giving the name of the book, the chapter of the book, and the verse: so for instance "Proverbs 8:7-8" means "the book called Proverbs, chapter eight, verses seven and eight". Translators may not agree about how to translate a passage, but at least they all use more or less the same numbering of chapters and verses.

A NOTE ON CHRISTIANITY

The Christian religion has its roots in an older religion that we call Judaism, the religion of the Jewish people. Its founder was a Jewish man known in his lifetime as Yeshua ha-Notsri, "Yeshua from the town of Nazareth". English-speaking Christians call him "Jesus", which is the Latin form of the name "Yeshua". Since they believe that he was God, they also call him "Christ", a Greek word meaning "a man who has been anointed as a king". (I ought to add that many Christians disagree strongly with each other about exactly what it means to say that Yeshua was or is God.) In this booklet I refer to Yeshua as Jesus, this being the standard form in English-speaking countries.

In the New Testament you can see how the early Church tended to split up into sects and pressure-groups. For several hundred years the Church was continually shaken by furious disputes about doctrine, about ceremonies, about who exactly Jesus was, about the nature of God, and about the Bible.

A thousand years after Jesus's death there was a new, massive, split, and the Eastern Church (Greek Orthodox) separated from the Western European Church (Roman Catholic). Five hundred years later still, the various Protestant churches also split away from the Roman Church. The Protestant churches now include the Baptists, the Methodists, the United Reformed Church, the Lutherans, the Quakers and the Anglican Church (which includes not only the Church of England but many other churches around the world). The Jehovah's Witnesses, Seventh Day Adventists, Plymouth Brethren, Exclusive Brethren, Assemblies of God, Christian Scientists, and Mormons also have roots in the Protestant tradition.

The word 'evangelical' refers not a single church, but to a 'conservative' wing or pressure-group whose members are spread across many of the Protestant churches. Evangelicals are strongly committed to studying the Bible in great detail. Unfortunately many of them do so in English, which means that they are especially vulnerable to being misled by the errors and inadequacies of whatever translations they happen to be using.

Another important technical word is 'sacrament'. A sacrament is a Christian religious ritual where a priest or minister uses a material substance to convey a special divine grace to someone else. *Baptism* is a sacrament, using water as the material substance. The *Eucharist* (also known as the *Lord's Supper*, the *Communion*, and the *Mass*) is another sacrament, using bread and wine. The churches don't entirely agree about which ceremonies are sacraments and which aren't. One sacrament that the churches do tend to agree about nowadays is, oddly, one that is both new-fangled and theologically questionable: *Marriage.*[1]

NOTES

1   For marriage, see section **2.3** above.